한은정 Berklee College of Music 졸업 / 현 정이조 영어학원 듣기 전문 강사
정수진 Temple University M. A. in TESOL / 현 정이조 영어학원 듣기, 말하기 전문 강사
김민호 선문대학교 통번역대학원 한영과 석사 / 현 김민호 영어학원 원장

English Conversation Training
Situation Drill 3

지은이 한은정, 정수진, 김민호
펴낸이 정규도
펴낸곳 (주)다락원

초판 1쇄 인쇄 2007년 8월 5일
초판 8쇄 발행 2024년 7월 18일

책임편집 김명진
영문교열 Michael A. Putlack
디자인 윤지은

다락원 경기도 파주시 문발로 211
내용문의: (02)736-2031 내선 503
구입문의: (02)736-2031 내선 250~252
Fax: (02)732-2037
출판등록 1977년 9월 16일 제406-2008-000007호

Copyright ⓒ 2007, 김민호

저자 및 출판사의 허락 없이 이 책의 일부 또는 전부를 무단 복제·전재·발췌할 수 없습니다. 구입 후 철회는 회사 내규에 부합하는 경우에 가능하므로 구입문의처에 문의하시기 바랍니다. 분실·파손 등에 따른 소비자 피해에 대해서는 공정거래위원회에서 고시한 소비자 분쟁 해결 기준에 따라 보상 가능합니다. 잘못된 책은 바꿔 드립니다.

ISBN 978-89-5995-914-3 58740

http://www.darakwon.co.kr
- 다락원 홈페이지를 방문하시면 상세한 출판정보와 함께 동영상강좌, MP3자료 등 다양한 어학 정보를 얻으실 수 있습니다.

한은정 · 정수진 · 김민호 지음

이 책을 시작하며

국제화, 세계화의 시대인 지금, 글로벌 언어인 영어의 중요성은 날이 갈수록 강조되고 있습니다. 그러나 우리는 의사소통을 원활히 할 수 있는 언어로서의 영어를 배우기보다는 단순히 시험문제를 풀기 위한 영어를 배워온 것이 사실입니다. 많은 학습자들이 영어 시험 점수는 높아도 실제 영어 회화를 어렵고 부담스럽게 느끼는 이유이죠.

이제는 시험용 암기만으로 끝나는 영어 공부가 아니라 언어로서 이해하고 실생활에서 사용할 수 있도록 한 걸음 더 내딛는 훈련이 필요합니다. 무조건 어려운 문장들을 암기하는 것은 실제 상황에서는 쓸 수 없기도 하고 기억하기도 힘듭니다. 〈English Conversation Training – Situation Drill 1, 2, 3, 4〉는 상황별로 실생활에서 자주 이용되는 쉽고 단순한 표현들 위주로 구성되어 있습니다. Situation Drill 1은 초·중등학생, Situation Drill 3은 고등학생들을 위한 실용적인 영어 표현들을 학습하게 하였고, Situation Drill 2에서는 외국으로 유학을 가는 학생들이 현지 도착부터 그쪽 생활에 익숙해질 때까지 꼭 필요한 일상생활 표현들을 다루었습니다. Situation Drill 4는 IBT TOEFL Speaking의 입문 단계로, 토플 준비 훈련이 될만한 문장 표현 익히기에 초점을 맞추고 있습니다.

영어는 하나의 언어이기 때문에 생활 속에서 지속적으로 익히는 것이 매우 중요합니다. 음원을 매일 반복적으로 들으면서 상황별 대화를 이해한다면 실생활에서도 쉽게 적용하여 사용할 수 있을 것입니다.

저자

Situation Drill_3

unit 1	**My computer is too slow.** 내 컴퓨터는 너무 느려요.	• 8
unit 2	**What's on TV?** TV에서 뭐 하나요?	• 10
unit 3	**I'm planning to have a birthday party.** 내 생일 파티를 하려고 해요.	• 12
unit 4	**Christmas is drawing near.** 크리스마스가 다가오네요.	• 14
unit 5	**What's the weather supposed to be like?** 날씨는 어떤가요?	• 16
unit 6	**Did you finish cleaning your room?** 방 청소는 다 했니?	• 18
unit 7	**Breakfast is ready.** 아침 다 됐다.	• 20
unit 8	**I feel like I'm coming down with a cold.** 감기에 걸릴 것 같아요.	• 22
unit 9	**Who's calling?** 누구세요?	• 24
unit 10	**I'd like to have a pet.** 애완동물을 기르고 싶어요.	• 26
unit 11	**You look happy today.** 너 오늘 기분 좋아 보인다.	• 28
unit 12	**You must be kidding.** 농담하는 거지?	• 30
unit 13	**I can't tell you how sorry I am.** 정말 미안해.	• 32
unit 14	**I'm seeing somebody now.** 나 요즘 사귀는 사람 있어.	• 34
unit 15	**Please don't lose your temper.** 흥분하지 마.	• 36
unit 16	**What they are saying about her is true.** 그녀에 대한 소문이 사실이구나.	• 38
unit 17	**I've got to get in shape.** 운동을 좀 해야겠어.	• 40
unit 18	**My school uniform is too loose.** 내 교복은 너무 헐렁해.	• 42
unit 19	**What are you into?** 취미가 뭐니?	• 44
unit 20	**Are you good at taking pictures?** 너 사진 잘 찍니?	• 46

Contents

unit 21	**What kind of musical was it?** 어떤 종류의 뮤지컬이었는데? • 48
unit 22	**I'll call the roll first.** 우선 출석을 부를게. • 50
unit 23	**Are you ready for the exam?** 시험 공부 많이 했니? • 52
unit 24	**I messed up the exam.** 나 시험 망쳤어. • 54
unit 25	**We're running out of gas.** 휘발유가 다 떨어져가네. • 56
unit 26	**Where are you headed?** 어디 가니? • 58
unit 27	**Is it close by?** 여기서 가깝나요? • 60
unit 28	**It's been a long time.** 진짜 오랜만이다. • 62
unit 29	**How often does the subway come?** 지하철은 얼마나 자주 오나요? • 64
unit 30	**May I take your order now?** 지금 주문하시겠어요? • 66
unit 31	**I can't eat another bite.** 더 이상은 못 먹겠어. • 68
unit 32	**This book is out now.** 이 책은 대출 중입니다. • 70
unit 33	**What seems to be the problem?** 어디가 아프신가요? • 72
unit 34	**Could you fill this prescription for me?** 약을 조제해 주시겠어요? • 74
unit 35	**How would you like to have your hair done?** 머리를 어떻게 해드릴까요? • 76
unit 36	**I'd like to open an account.** 은행 계좌를 열고 싶은데요. • 78
unit 37	**Are you a Christian?** 너 기독교 신자니? • 80
unit 38	**This is my first time to take a plane.** 비행기 타는 건 처음이야. • 82
unit 39	**This package contains books and pictures.** 이 소포의 내용물은 책과 사진들입니다. • 84
unit 40	**Do you have any particular style in mind?** 특별히 생각해 두신 스타일이 있나요? • 86

unit 1 | My computer is too slow.
내 컴퓨터는 너무 느려요.

Dialog

Dad Why the long face? You look like something is bothering you.

Eileen Yes, Dad. I need to use the computer to finish my project, but my computer is too slow. And there's something wrong with it, too.

Dad What's wrong with the computer? Is it serious?

Eileen My computer sometimes turns off while I'm in the middle of my work.

Dad Oh, no. That's really bad. I think we need to fix it right away.

Eileen Yeah, it's painful for me to save the files every 5 minutes.

Dad Let's take the computer to the service center on Saturday and get it fixed.

---

long face 수심이 가득한 얼굴　　**bother** 괴롭히다
serious 심각한, 중대한　　**painful** 힘드는

Situation Drill Level 3

Let's Speak!

아빠   왜 그렇게 시무룩하니? 뭔가 문제가 있어 보이는구나.
아일린   네, 아빠. 프로젝트를 끝내려면 컴퓨터를 써야 하는데 컴퓨터가 너무 느려요. 그리고 문제도 좀 있어요.
아빠   컴퓨터에 무슨 문제가 있는 거니? 심각하니?
아일린   컴퓨터가 사용하는 도중에 종종 꺼져버리곤 해요.
아빠   맙소사. 그거 정말 큰일이구나. 내 생각엔 빨리 컴퓨터를 고쳐야 할 것 같은데.
아일린   네. 5분마다 파일들을 저장해야 해서 정말 힘들어요.
아빠   토요일에 컴퓨터를 서비스 센터에 가져가서 고치도록 하자.

Learn More

1. **I bought this sweater on the Internet.**
   나는 이 스웨터를 인터넷에서 샀어.

2. **Can you help me use this software?**
   이 프로그램 쓰는 방법 좀 알려 줄래?

3. **I think your computer has a virus.**
   네 컴퓨터가 바이러스에 감염된 것 같아.

4. **Can you tell me how to get it printed?**
   프린트는 어떻게 하는지 좀 알려 줄래?

unit 2 | What's on TV?
TV에서 뭐 하나요?

Dialog

Glen   Mom, what's on TV?

Mom   This is my favorite drama. I take delight in watching this drama on TV every Monday and Tuesday night.

Glen   Well, I enjoy watching a professional baseball game. What time does that drama end?

Mom   It will end in 10 minutes. Is there anything good on another channel?

Glen   The baseball game is on another channel.

Mom   What channel is it on?

Glen   It's on channel 11. After you finish watching the drama, give me the remote, please.

Mom   Okay, I will do that.

---

favorite 매우 좋아하는   **professional** 프로의
delight 기쁨, 즐거움

Situation Drill Level 3

Let's Speak!

글렌 엄마, TV에서 뭐 해요?
엄마 내가 제일 좋아하는 드라마란다. 매주 월요일과 화요일 밤에 이 드라마를 보는 것을 즐거움으로 삼고 있지.
글렌 음, 저는 프로야구 중계를 보는 것을 좋아해요. 그 드라마는 몇 시에 끝나요?
엄마 10분 안에 끝날 건데, 다른 데서 뭐 재미있는 거라도 하니?
글렌 다른 채널에서 야구 경기를 하거든요.
엄마 어떤 채널인데?
글렌 채널 11번에서 해요. 드라마 다 보신 후에 리모컨을 제게 주세요.
엄마 그래, 그렇게 하마.

Learn More

1. **Does she enjoy television broadcasts every night?**
   그녀는 매일 저녁 텔레비전을 봅니까?

2. **You're such a couch potato.** 넌 어떻게 항상 TV만 보고 사니?

3. **You're sitting too close to the TV.** TV앞에 너무 가까이 앉았구나.

4. **What do you want to watch?** 뭐 볼래?

unit 3 | I'm planning to have a birthday party. 내 생일 파티를 하려고 해요.

Dialog

Eileen   Dad, I'm planning to have a birthday party this weekend. Would that be okay with you?

Dad   Sure! Are you going to invite your friends from school?

Eileen   Most of them will be my school friends. And I'll also invite some of my church friends.

Dad   Then, how many of your friends will be here?

Eileen   Well, I'm thinking of having about 20 friends here.

Dad   All right. By the way, what do you want for your birthday?

Eileen   Wow, you'll get a present for me? Thank you, Dad. There's one thing I have in mind.

Dad   I see. I'll talk to your Mom and get something for you.

Eileen   Thank you, Dad.

---

have in mind ~을 마음에 간직하다

Situation Drill Level 3

Let's Speak!

아일린   아빠, 이번 주말에 제 생일 파티를 하려고 해요. 괜찮을까요?
아빠   물론이지! 학교 친구들을 초대할 거니?
아일린   대부분이 학교 친구들이에요. 그리고 교회 친구들도 몇 명 초대할까 해요.
아빠   그럼 몇 명의 친구들이 올 예정이니?
아일린   음, 대략 20명 정도 생각하고 있어요.
아빠   알겠다. 근데, 생일 선물로 뭘 받고 싶니?
아일린   와, 생일 선물 사주시려고요? 고맙습니다, 아빠. 생각해 놓은 것이 한 가지 있기는 해요.
아빠   알았다. 네 엄마와 얘기해 보고 사주도록 하마.
아일린   감사합니다, 아빠.

Learn More

1. **I feel as though I'm on top of the world.**   기분이 날아갈 것만 같아.

2. **I'm so glad we see things eye to eye.**   서로 마음이 통해서 기뻐요.

unit 4 | Christmas is drawing near.
크리스마스가 다가오네요.

Dialog

Glen   I'm so excited because Christmas is drawing near.

Mom   Christmas is a very happy day for children because they get presents from their parents on Christmas.

Glen   Oh, my friend already gave me these mittens for Christmas present yesterday.

Mom   Good for you. They're really cute. Did you also give something to your friend?

Glen   Yes. I gave her a muffler. She liked it very much.

Mom   There are only a few days left in the year. What do you want to do on the last day of the year?

Glen   I'll be busy getting through all the things I want to do before the year is over. I'll also have to make some plans for the new year.

Mom   And don't forget that we have to visit the other members of our family in the morning on New Year's Day.

---

draw (때가) 가까워지다
muffler 목도리
make plans 계획을 세우다

mittens 벙어리 장갑
get through ~을 끝내다, 마치다

Situation Drill Level 3

Let's Speak!

글렌   크리스마스가 다가오니 너무 신나네요.

엄마   아이들은 크리스마스 때 부모님께 선물을 받으니 아이들에게는 매우 즐거운 날이지.

글렌   아, 어제 친구가 크리스마스 선물로 벌써 이 벙어리 장갑을 줬어요.

엄마   좋겠구나. 너무 귀여운 장갑이다. 너도 네 친구에게 뭘 줬니?

글렌   네. 목도리를 줬어요. 너무 좋아하던걸요.

엄마   금년도 며칠 안 남았구나. 올해의 마지막 날에 뭘 하고 싶니?

글렌   올해가 가기 전에 하고 싶은 일들을 마무리 하느라 바쁠 거예요. 또한 새해를 위한 계획도 세워야 할 테고요.

엄마   그리고 새해 아침에 친척집을 방문해야 하는 것도 잊지 말아라.

Learn More

1. We've decorated the Christmas tree in the living room.
   우리는 거실에 크리스마스 트리 장식을 했어요.

2. We eat rice-cake soup, called dduk-guk, on New Year's Day. 우리는 설날에 떡국을 먹습니다.

unit 5 | What's the weather supposed to be like? 날씨는 어떤가요?

Dialog

Glen   What's the weather supposed to be like tomorrow?

Mom   The weather forecast says it will drop below freezing tomorrow. And there's also a chance of snow.

Glen   I can't stand this cold weather. I wonder when spring will come.

Mom   The weather forecast says that the cold spell will end this weekend.

Glen   That's a relief. But now I think I need to turn on the heater.

Mom   When I was young, it was much colder than nowadays, and it often snowed. I enjoyed making snowmen with my friends.

Glen   I like to have snowball fights when it snows. But I don't like to shovel snow.

Mom   You know that we should shovel the snow in front of our house. If we don't, it would be pretty dangerous for people to walk on the street.

---

weather forecast 일기 예보
spell (날씨 등이 지속되는) 기간
heater 난방 장치
shovel ~을 삽으로 파다
below freezing 영하의
relief 안심
nowadays 오늘날

Situation Drill Level 3

Let's Speak!

글렌 내일 날씨는 어떤가요?
엄마 일기 예보에서 내일은 영하로 떨어질 거라더구나. 그리고 눈이 올 수도 있단다.
글렌 난 이렇게 추운 날씨는 정말 싫어요. 언제나 봄이 올까요?
엄마 일기 예보에서 이번 주말에는 날이 풀릴 거라고 하더구나.
글렌 다행이네요. 하지만 지금은 히터를 좀 틀어야겠어요.
엄마 엄마가 어렸을 때는 요즘보다 더 춥고 눈이 자주 왔단다. 친구들과 눈사람도 만들고 재미있었지.
글렌 눈이 오면 눈싸움을 할 수 있어 좋아요. 하지만 눈을 치우는 건 싫어요.
엄마 우리 집 앞의 눈은 우리가 치워야 한다는 걸 알잖니. 그렇지 않으면 길이 미끄러워 사람들에게 위험할 거야.

Learn More

1. **It's hot and humid.** 날씨가 후덥지근하군.

2. **You keep saying, "It's cold."** 춥다는 말이 입에 뱄구나.

3. **It's likely to rain.** 비가 올 것 같아요.

4. **It's getting a little cloudy.** 날이 흐려지기 시작했어요.

5. **It's pretty cold this morning, isn't it?** 오늘 아침은 꽤 춥네요, 그렇죠?

unit 6 | Did you finish cleaning your room? 방 청소는 다 했니?

Dialog

Glen   Mom, I'm going out to see some friends.

Mom   Did you already finish cleaning your room? You told me that you would do that this weekend.

Glen   Oh, I totally forgot about it. Well, can I clean my room when I come back?

Mom   Not this time. Your room is really messy, and I'm telling you to put your things in order right now.

Glen   But I'm not the only one who made this mess. Eileen always comes to my room and messes up things.

Mom   Oh, come on, Glen. Are you blaming your little sister now? Shame on you! You are the one who has to be responsible. Now go back to your room, and clean it before you go out. Okay?

Glen   Well, I see. But please tell Eileen not to touch anything in my room unless she puts it back in the same spot.

Mom   All right. I'll tell her that.

---

messy 지저분한
blame 탓하다, 책임을 지우다
spot (특정) 장소
put in order 정리하다
shame 부끄러워하다
responsible 책임이 있는

Situation Drill Level 3

Let's Speak!

글렌   엄마, 저 친구들 만나러 나가요.
엄마   방 청소는 벌써 끝낸 거니? 이번 주말에는 청소한다고 했잖니.
글렌   아, 완전히 잊고 있었어요. 돌아와서 청소하면 안 될까요?
엄마   이번엔 안 된다. 방이 너무 지저분하니 어서 정리하도록 해라.
글렌   하지만 제가 다 지저분하게 한 건 아니라고요. 아일린이 항상 제 방에 와서 어지럽히는 건데요.
엄마   맙소사, 글렌. 지금 여동생 탓을 하고 있는 거니? 부끄러운 줄 알아라! 네게 책임이 있는 거란다. 어서 방으로 가서 정리하고 나가거라. 알겠니?
글렌   네, 알겠어요. 하지만 아일린에게 제 방에 와서 쓴 물건을 제자리에 놓지 않을 거면 건드리지 말라고 얘기해 주세요.
엄마   그래. 얘기하마.

Learn More

1. **Please dust the furniture everyday.** 가구의 먼지는 매일 털어내렴.

2. **I'll do the dishes.** 설거지는 제가 할게요.

3. **I need to do some laundry.** 빨래할 게 좀 있어요.

unit 7 | Breakfast is ready.
아침 다 됐다.

Dialog

Mom   Glen! Breakfast is ready.

Glen   I'm coming. Did you have a good night's sleep, Mom?

Mom   Yes. Thanks. How about you?

Glen   Me, too. It smells great. It's making me hungry now.

Mom   Could you bring the cups and milk to the table? The milk is on the top shelf in the refrigerator.

Glen   Shall I pour some milk into each cup?

Mom   Yes, please. Here are some ham and eggs. Do you want some toast?

Glen   That would be good. And I need the strawberry jam.

Mom   Here you go. Help yourself, please. There's more toast, so tell me if you want some more.

Glen   It's enough. Thank you, Mom. Everything is really delicious.

---

shelf 선반   **refrigerator** 냉장고
pour 따르다   **delicious** 맛있는

Situation Drill Level 3

Let's Speak!

엄마	글렌! 아침 다 됐다.
글렌	가요. 엄마, 안녕히 주무셨어요?
엄마	그래, 고맙구나. 너는 잘 잤니?
글렌	네, 잘 잤어요. 냄새가 아주 좋아요. 냄새 때문에 배가 고파지네요.
엄마	컵과 우유를 테이블에 가져다 주겠니? 우유는 냉장고 맨 위 칸에 있단다.
글렌	우유를 컵에 따라 놓을까요?
엄마	그래. 여기 햄과 계란이 있다. 토스트도 먹을래?
글렌	네, 맛있겠네요. 그리고 딸기잼도 좀 주세요.
엄마	여기 있다. 맛있게 먹으렴. 토스트가 더 있으니 좀 더 먹으려면 얘기하렴.
글렌	충분해요. 고마워요, 엄마. 다 진짜 맛있네요.

Learn More

1. **My mother is a world-class cook.** 우리 엄마 요리 솜씨는 세계 최고야.

2. **I've had enough.** 많이 먹었습니다.

3. **Don't eat too much.** 너무 과식하지 마세요.

4. **Do you like the dish?** 음식은 입맛에 맞나요?

unit 8 I feel like I'm coming down with a cold. 감기에 걸릴 것 같아요.

Dialog

Glen Mom, I feel like I am coming down with a cold.

Mom You should be careful of colds when the seasons change.

Glen Do you think I'd better take some medicine for this cold?

Mom Do you have a runny nose?

Glen No, I don't. But I have a stuffy nose.

Mom Then what about your throat?

Glen My throat hurts when I swallow food.

Mom I think you'd better go to see a doctor before it gets worse. Nowadays, it's common to get the flu. I hope you feel better soon.

Glen Okay, Mom. I'll do that.

---

come down with (병에) 걸리다
sore throat 인후염
flu 유행성 감기
runny nose 콧물이 흐르는 코
swallow 삼키다, 들이키다

Situation Drill Level 3

Let's Speak!

글렌　　엄마, 저 감기에 걸릴 것 같아요.
엄마　　환절기에는 감기에 조심해야 해.
글렌　　감기약을 먹는 게 나을까요?
엄마　　콧물이 나니?
글렌　　아니요. 하지만 코가 막혔어요.
엄마　　그럼 목은 어떠니?
글렌　　음식을 삼킬 때 목이 아파요.
엄마　　더 심해지기 전에 병원에 가보는 게 좋을 것 같구나. 요즘 감기가 유행이라는데 말이다. 빨리 좋아졌으면 좋겠다.
글렌　　네, 엄마. 그럴게요.

Learn More

1. **I blew my nose all day long.** 하루 종일 코를 풀었어요.

2. **He has had a cough all night.** 그는 밤새 기침을 했어요.

3. **I have a cold and am sneezing a lot.** 감기에 걸려 재채기가 많이 납니다.

4. **She's had this cold for over a week.**
   그녀는 일주일 넘게 감기를 앓고 있어요.

unit 9 | Who's calling?
누구세요?

Dialog

Glen   Hello. Is Jenny there?

Jenny   This is she. Who's calling?

Glen   Hi, this is Glen. Are you free this weekend?

Jenny   I've got no particular plans yet. Why?

Glen   That's great. Let's catch a movie this weekend.

Jenny   Which movie are you planning to watch?

Glen   *Spiderman 3* is showing now. I've been waiting for a long time. Have you watched *Spiderman 1* and *2*?

Jenny   Yes, I have. Those were pretty cool as I remember.

Glen   All right. Let's get tickets for that movie. First, I have to check the schedule for the movie.

Jenny   Why don't you check on the Internet and see what time the movie is playing?

Glen   That's a good idea. I'll check and call you back.

---

particular 특별한   catch (연극, 영화 등을) 보다

Situation Drill Level 3

Let's Speak!

글렌 여보세요. 제니 있나요?
제니 제가 제니인데요. 누구세요?
글렌 안녕, 나 글렌이야. 이번 주말에 시간 있니?
제니 아직 다른 계획이 없긴 한데, 왜?
글렌 잘됐다. 주말에 영화나 보러 가자.
제니 무슨 영화 보려고 하는데?
글렌 〈스파이더맨 3〉가 하고 있어. 난 오랫동안 기다려 왔거든. 〈스파이더맨 1, 2〉 편 봤니?
제니 응, 봤어. 내가 기억하기론 그 영화들 재미있었어.
글렌 좋았어! 그 영화 티켓 사자. 우선 영화 시간표를 알아 봐야 해.
제니 인터넷으로 확인해서 몇 시에 있는지 알아 보는 게 어때?
글렌 좋은 생각이다. 내가 확인해 보고 다시 전화할게.

Learn More

1. **Are you listening to me?** 제 말을 듣고 계신가요?

2. **Your voice keeps fading.** 목소리가 점점 안 들려요.

3. **What's that noise?** 이 잡음은 뭐죠?

unit 10 | I'd like to have a pet.
애완동물을 기르고 싶어요.

Dialog

Eileen Dad, I'd like to have a pet. Is that okay?

Dad Well, we need to think about it. Having a pet means a lot of responsibility.

Eileen I know. I'll be the one who's in charge of taking care of him. I'll also walk the dog everyday.

Dad If you insist, that would be okay with me. Then what kind of pet do you think you want to have?

Eileen I've been thinking about getting a puppy as my first pet. I'd love to have a cat also, but, since I am allergic to cats, I don't think it's a good idea to have a pet cat.

Dad That's right. I'd rather have a dog. They are very friendly and faithful.

Eileen I have a friend who has a pet porcupine.

Dad Really? Oh, that's really interesting. But I think it must be very difficult to pet it.

---

pet 애완동물, ~을 쓰다듬다
in charge of ~을 맡고 있는, 담당의
allergic 알레르기 체질의
porcupine 고슴도치
responsibility 책임감
take care of ~을 돌보다
faithful 충실한

Situation Drill Level 3

Let's Speak!

아일린 아빠, 저 애완동물을 기르고 싶어요. 괜찮을까요?
아빠 글쎄다, 생각 좀 해보자꾸나. 애완동물을 기르려면 그만큼의 책임도 필요하단다.
아일린 알아요. 제가 다 알아서 기를게요. 매일 산책도 시킬 거예요.
아빠 네가 그렇게까지 하겠다면 괜찮을 거 같구나. 그럼 어떤 애완동물을 키우고 싶은 거니?
아일린 생각해 봤는데요, 강아지가 저의 첫 번째 애완동물로 좋을 것 같아요. 고양이도 생각해 봤는데 알레르기가 있어서 고양이를 기르는 것은 좋은 생각이 아닌 것 같아요.
아빠 그래. 나도 개가 더 나을 것 같다. 개들은 친근하고 충성스럽거든.
아일린 제 친구는 애완동물로 고슴도치를 키워요.
아빠 그래? 정말 흥미롭구나. 하지만 쓰다듬기는 힘들 것 같구나.

Learn More

1. **May I pet the dog?** 개를 쓰다듬어도 되나요?

2. **No pets are allowed.** 애완동물은 허용되지 않습니다.

3. **What do I have to feed it?** 무슨 먹이를 줘야 하나요?

unit 11 | You look happy today.
너 오늘 기분 좋아 보인다.

Dialog

Eilleen You look so happy today. What's the occasion?

Victor I have some good news. I won the competition.

Eilleen Congratulations! I'm happy for you. What kind of competition was it?

Victor It was an English speech competition. I prepared for it for 3 months.

Eilleen You must be very proud of yourself.

Victor I'm so excited I can't do anything. I think things couldn't be better. Let's go out for dinner. It's on me.

Eilleen Wow, that's great. Let's go to a Chinese restaurant.

---

occasion 경우, 특별한 일 **competition** 경쟁, 시합
prepare for ~을 준비하다

Situation Drill Level 3

Let's Speak!

아일린 너 오늘 기분 좋아 보이는데, 무슨 일이니?
빅터 좋은 소식이 있어. 경연 대회에서 우승했거든.
아일린 축하해! 정말 잘됐다. 무슨 경연 대회였는데?
빅터 영어 발표 경연 대회였어. 난 3개월 동안 준비했었지.
아일린 굉장히 뿌듯하겠다.
빅터 너무 들떠서 아무것도 못할 정도야. 이보다 더 좋을 순 없을 것 같아. 저녁 먹으러 나가자. 내가 살게.
아일린 와, 멋진데. 중국 음식점으로 가자.

Learn More

1. **I'm glad you could drop by.** 들러 줘서 고마워.

2. **It really made me happy.** 그것 때문에 정말 행복했어.

3. **They're like two lovebirds.** 그들은 깨가 쏟아지더라.

unit 12 | You must be kidding.
농담하는 거지?

Dialog

Eileen Is there something on my face?

Victor No. But you look a little different today.

Eileen Oh, that's because of my new glasses. How do I look?

Victor They look great on you. You look younger in them.

Eileen That's very nice of you. Just between the two of us, I'm concerned about my appearance these days.

Victor You must be kidding. You are already really good-looking.

Eileen Are you flirting with me? Don't make fun of me, okay?

Victor I'm sorry if I made you feel bad. But I'm serious that you don't have to worry too much about your appearance.

---

concern 걱정하다, 염려하다
flirt 장난 삼아 연애하다, (이성과) 시시덕거리다
appearance 외모
make fun of 놀리다

Situation Drill Level 3

Let's Speak!

아일린　내 얼굴에 뭐 묻었니?
빅터　아니, 근데 오늘 뭔가 달라 보이는데.
아일린　아, 내 새 안경 때문인가 보다. 어때?
빅터　너무 잘 어울린다. 더 어려 보이는 걸.
아일린　정말 고마워. 우리끼리 있으니깐 말인데, 나 요즘 외모에 신경 좀 쓰고 있어.
빅터　농담하는 거지? 넌 이미 정말 예뻐.
아일린　나한테 작업 거는 거니? 놀리지 말아줘.
빅터　기분 상하게 했다면 미안해. 하지만 네 외모에 너무 신경 쓰지 않아도 된다는 건 진심이야.

Learn More

1. **She has a big mouth.** 그 여자는 입이 너무 싸.

2. **You can't judge a book by its cover.** 겉만 보고 판단하면 안 돼.

unit 13 | I can't tell you how sorry I am.

정말 미안해.

Dialog

Glen Jenny, I must ask for your forgiveness.

Jenny What's wrong?

Glen I lost the notebook which you lent me last week. I should have paid more attention.

Jenny Oh my God. I didn't make a copy of it, so now I don't know what to study with.

Glen I can't tell you how sorry I am. It's all my fault. It was raining, and I had too much stuff in my hands. I probably dropped it somewhere on my way home. It won't happen again.

Jenny I don't want to hear any excuses. My midterm exam is coming, and I'm in big trouble now.

Glen But the good thing is that I already made a copy of your notes. Now will you accept my apology?

Jenny That's a relief to hear. All right. As long as you have copied it, I'll be able to study for the midterm.

---

fault 잘못
excuse 변명
relief 안심, 안도

stuff 물건
midterm exam 중간고사

Situation Drill Level 3

Let's Speak!

글렌　제니, 네게 사과를 해야겠어.
제니　무슨 일이야?
글렌　지난 주에 네가 빌려 준 공책을 잃어버렸어. 내가 더 주의를 했어야 했는데 말이야.
제니　이런. 난 공책을 복사해 두지 못했는데, 이제 무얼 보고 공부해야 할지 모르겠네.
글렌　정말 미안해. 다 내 잘못이야. 비가 오는데 손에 든 물건들이 너무 많았거든. 아마 집에 가는 길목에 떨어뜨렸나 봐. 다시는 그런 일은 없을 거야.
제니　변명은 듣고 싶지 않아. 중간고사가 다가오고 있는데 큰일이라고.
글렌　하지만 다행히도 네가 기록한 걸 이미 복사해 두었어. 그럼 이젠 내 사과를 받아 주겠니?
제니　그 말을 들으니 안심이다. 알았어. 공책이 복사되어 있다면, 나는 중간고사 공부를 할 수 있겠다.

unit 14 | I'm seeing somebody now.
나 요즘 사귀는 사람 있어.

Dialog

Jenny Hey, do you have anything scheduled for tomorrow?
Victor I've got a previous engagement.
Jenny How about the day after tomorrow?
Victor Well, I guess I have to tell you the truth. I'm seeing somebody now.
Jenny Wow, congratulations! How did you meet her?
Victor I met her on a blind date. I fell in love with her at first sight.
Jenny It sounds like she's something else.
Victor There's a lot about her to love. She's so sweet.

---

previous 앞의, 이전의
blind date 안면이 없는 남녀의 데이트, 미팅
sweet 상냥한
engagement 약속(= appointment)
at first sight 첫눈에

Situation Drill Level 3

Let's Speak!

제니 내일 스케줄 잡은 거 있니?
빅터 선약이 있어.
제니 모레는 어때?
빅터 사실을 말해야 할 것 같다. 나 요즘 사귀는 사람 있어.
제니 와, 축하해. 어떻게 만나게 된 거야?
빅터 소개팅에서 만났어. 완전 첫눈에 반했다니까.
제니 대단한 여자인가 보네.
빅터 그녀는 사랑스러운 점이 많아. 애교도 많고.

Learn More

1. **She's really popular.** 그녀는 인기가 정말 많아.

2. **He's difficult to get along with.** 그는 정말 사귀기 힘들어.

3. **She's dating someone younger than herself.**
   그녀는 연하랑 사귀는 중이야.

unit 15 | Please don't lose your temper.
홍분하지 마.

Dialog

Glen   This is too much.

Jenny   What's wrong with you?

Glen   I'm tired of doing this. I've been revising this for the entire week.

Jenny   Isn't this your project? It looks great to me.

Glen   I was supposed to finish this project last week, but then my teacher told me to do some more research. But it's taking a lot of time to reorganize it.

Jenny   Please don't lose your temper. Don't take it out on me.

Glen   Oh, I'm sorry. I always try to keep cool, but I sometimes lose my temper.

Jenny   Get a hold of yourself. If there is anything that I can do to help you, just tell me.

Glen   Oh, thank you for cheering me up.

---

revise 수정, 수정하다
reorganize 재정리하다
lose one's temper 화가 머리끝까지 나다
entire 전체의
take out on ~에게 분풀이를 하다
cheer up 격려하다

Situation Drill Level 3

Let's Speak!

글렌　이건 너무해.
제니　무슨 일이니?
글렌　난 더 이상 이 일은 하기 싫어. 이번 주 내내 난 이걸 수정하고 있다고.
제니　그거 네 프로젝트 아니니? 나한텐 괜찮아 보이는데.
글렌　지난 주까지 이 프로젝트를 마쳤어야 하는데, 선생님께서 몇 가지 조사를 더 하라고 하셔서 말이야. 하지만 이걸 다시 정리하는 데 정말 오래 걸리고 있어.
제니　흥분하지 마. 내게 화풀이하지 말라고.
글렌　아, 미안해. 항상 냉정하려고 하지만 가끔 흥분하곤 해.
제니　힘내! 내가 도와줄 수 있는 게 있으면 말해.
글렌　격려해 줘서 고마워.

Learn More

1. **Stop getting on my nerves.** 신경 건드리지 말아 줘.

2. **Give me a break.** 한번만 봐줘.

3. **Why are you picking on me?** 왜 나만 가지고 그래?

4. **It's none of your business.** 너와는 상관 없어.

unit 16 | What they are saying about her is true.

그녀에 대한 소문이 사실이구나.

Dialog

Jenny Do you mean it? What they're saying about her is true. But what made you so sure it's true?

Glen I heard it from the person herself.

Jenny Wow, are you close to her? She really trusts you very much.

Glen I'm sorry I couldn't tell you earlier. But I had no choice.

Jenny Don't worry. I understand that she must've told you to keep it a secret. She may not want her rivals to get any more information.

Glen Thank you for understanding. But this is for your eyes only, okay?

Jenny Sure. My lips are sealed.

---

keep ~ a secret ~을 비밀로 하다
eyes only 최고 기밀의
rival 경쟁자
sealed 봉인을 한

Situation Drill Level 3

Let's Speak!

제니   정말이야? 그 소문이 사실이구나. 근데 그게 사실인지 어떻게 알았어?
글렌   걔한테 직접 들었어.
제니   와, 너 걔랑 친하니? 널 정말 많이 믿나봐.
글렌   미리 말해 주지 못해서 미안해. 하지만 선택의 여지가 없었어.
제니   괜찮아. 걔가 비밀로 해달라고 했을 테니 이해해. 경쟁자들이 더 많은 정보를 얻는 걸 원치는 않았을 테니깐 말이야.
글렌   이해해 줘서 고마워. 하지만 이건 기밀 사항이야, 알겠지?
제니   물론이야. 비밀로 할게.

Learn More

1. **I give you my word.** 정말이야.

2. **She can't do such a thing.** 걔가 그런 일을 할 리 없어.

3. **Don't worry. I won't tell anyone.** 걱정 마. 아무한테도 얘기 안 할게.

4. **If I were you, I would be careful about what I say.**
   내가 너라면, 말 조심 할 거야.

unit 17 | I've got to get in shape.
운동을 좀 해야겠어.

Dialog

Victor　You look like you have lost some weight.

Eileen　Can you notice that? I lost 3kg last month.

Victor　Good for you. I've put on a little weight. I've got to get in shape.

Eileen　I work out 3 times a week. I was so sore from working out for the first couple of days. But I got used to it later.

Victor　I heard that it's important to warm up before working out.

Eileen　That's right. You should do some stretching exercises first. And if you want to lose weight, you should exercise regularly.

Victor　Thank you for your advice. I'll start exercising to maintain my health and lose weight.

---

notice 알아채다
put on (체중을) 늘리다
sore 아픈, 쑤시는
Good for you! 잘됐다!
get in shape (운동으로) 몸이 좋아지다
warm up 준비 운동을 하다

Situation Drill Level 3

Let's Speak!

빅터 　너 살이 좀 빠진 것 같은데.
아일린 　알아 보겠니? 나 지난 달에 3kg을 뺐어.
빅터 　좋겠다. 나는 살이 좀 쪘어. 몸을 만들어야겠어.
아일린 　난 일주일에 3일 운동해. 처음 며칠 동안은 운동 때문에 몸이 쑤시고 아팠어. 하지만 나중엔 괜찮아졌어.
빅터 　운동 전에 몸을 푸는 것이 중요하다고 들었어.
아일린 　맞아. 먼저 스트레칭을 해줘야 해. 그리고 살을 빼고 싶다면 규칙적으로 운동을 해야 해.
빅터 　조언 고마워. 운동 시작해서 건강도 지키고 살도 빼야겠어.

Learn More

1. **I'm on a diet now.** 나는 지금 다이어트 중이야.

2. **You need to drink a lot of water.** 물을 많이 마셔야 해.

3. **I have a stiff shoulder.** 어깨가 뻐근해.

4. **You have to eat three meals a day.**
   하루에 세끼 식사를 챙겨 먹어야 해.

5. **You are in great shape.** 너 몸매(몸 상태)가 좋구나.

unit 18 | My school uniform is too loose.
내 교복은 너무 헐렁해.

Dialog

Eileen   I'm going to have my school uniform made today after school.

Jenny   I ordered mine yesterday. I'll buy some new shoes today.

Eileen   How did you make the length of the skirt?

Jenny   I wanted it short, but my skirt will be a little longer than I wanted because I will grow taller.

Eileen   Yeah, that's what my mother thinks, too. Well, as long as we have to wear it for 3 years, I guess she's right.

Jenny   But, during the first year, my school uniform will be too loose.

Eileen   I see some truth in what you are saying. Wish me luck on my school uniform. And I hope you get some nice shoes.

---

school uniform 교복   loose 헐거운, 느슨한

Situation Drill Level 3

Let's Speak!

아일린   나는 하교 후 교복 맞추러 갈 거야.
제니   내 것은 어제 주문했어. 오늘은 새 신발을 사러 갈 거야.
아일린   치마 길이는 어떻게 했니?
제니   나는 짧은 길이로 하고 싶었는데 키가 클 거니까 내가 원하는 것보다는 길게 주문했어.
아일린   그래, 우리 엄마도 그렇게 생각하셔. 하긴, 3년 동안 입어야 할 교복이니 엄마 말씀이 맞는 것 같아.
제니   하지만 1년 동안은 교복이 너무 헐렁할 거야.
아일린   네 말도 일리가 있어. 교복 잘 맞출 수 있게 행운을 빌어줘. 그리고 넌 멋진 신발 사길 바래.

Learn More

1. **When is the fitting?** 가봉은 언제야?

2. **Do you have this coat in my size?** 제게 맞는 사이즈의 코트가 있나요?

3. **I ordered my school uniform too tight.**
   나는 교복을 너무 꽉 끼게 주문했어.

4. **This fits me quite well. I will take this one.**
   이건 잘 맞는군요. 이것을 살게요.

5. **The jacket is a bit tight around the shoulders.**
   이 자켓은 어깨가 좀 끼네요.

unit 19 | What are you into?
취미가 뭐니?

Dialog

Victor   What are you into?

Eileen   I like reading books. I think I'm a bookworm.

Victor   What kinds of books do you like to read?

Eileen   I like mystery novels. Oh, I also enjoy detective novels.

Victor   How many books do you read a month?

Eileen   I read more than two books a month. What's your hobby?

Victor   I like hiking in the mountains. I went hiking last weekend with my family.

Eileen   Wow, that sounds interesting. I like outdoor sports, too.

Victor   Then why don't we go hiking together this weekend?

Eileen   Sounds like a good idea to me. Let's get some fresh air in the mountains.

---

into ~에 관심을 가지고, ~에 열중하여
mystery novel 추리 소설
outdoor 야외의
bookworm 책벌레
detective 탐정

Situation Drill Level 3

Let's Speak!

빅터   취미가 뭐니?
아일린   나는 책 읽는 것을 좋아해. 나는 책벌레인 것 같아.
빅터   어떤 종류의 책을 좋아하는데?
아일린   나는 추리 소설을 좋아해. 아, 탐정 소설도 좋아하고.
빅터   한 달에 몇 권의 책을 읽니?
아일린   한 달에 두 권 이상은 읽어. 너의 취미는 뭐니?
빅터   난 등산을 좋아해. 지난 주말에 식구들과 등산을 다녀왔어.
아일린   와, 재미있겠는걸. 나도 야외 스포츠를 좋아해.
빅터   그럼 이번 주말에 같이 등산 가는 게 어때?
아일린   좋은 생각인 것 같아. 산에 신선한 공기를 마시러 가자.

Learn More

1. **I have never gone skiing.**   나는 스키를 타본 적이 없어.

2. **How do you like to spend your free time?**   한가할 때는 뭘 하니?

3. **Do you go to the movies very often?**   영화를 자주 보러 가니?

4. **I've been collecting these foreign stamps for three years.**
   나는 3년 동안 외국 우표를 모으고 있어.

unit 20 | Are you good at taking pictures? 너 사진 잘 찍니?

Dialog

Glen My sister likes to spend her time snapping pictures of herself with her cellular phone camera.

Jenny My brother also takes his own pictures with his digital camera and even uploads them to the Internet.

Glen She tries out a variety of poses with the camera held high above her head. Most of her pictures look very pretty, but, as matter of fact, she has a little secret.

Jenny What is it?

Glen She uses photo software to make her pictures look better.

Jenny I like taking pictures of scenery but not of myself because I'm not photogenic.

Glen Are you good at taking pictures?

Jenny I'm not very good at it, but I enjoy taking pictures. Oh, a few months ago, I got a chance to take a picture of Hyori Lee at a restaurant.

Glen Does she look better in person?

Jenny Yes. She looks better in real life than in pictures. I'll show it to you later.

---

snap 찰깍하고 찍다
upload 자료를 전송하다
photogenic 사진을 잘 받는
cellular phone 휴대전화
scenery 풍경

Situation Drill Level 3

Let's Speak!

글렌　내 여동생은 휴대폰 카메라로 자기 사진을 찍으며 시간 보내길 좋아해.
제니　내 남동생도 디지털 카메라로 자기 사진을 찍어서 인터넷에 올리기까지 하더라고.
글렌　내 동생은 카메라를 머리 위로 들고 다양한 포즈들을 시도하더라. 걔 사진들은 대부분 예쁘게 나오는데, 사실은 비밀이 있어.
제니　그게 뭔데?
글렌　포토 소프트웨어를 사용해서 더 나아 보이게 만든다는 거야.
제니　난 풍경 사진 찍는 건 좋아하지만 난 사진이 잘 안 받아서 내 사진을 찍는 건 별로야.
글렌　너 사진 잘 찍니?
제니　그렇게 실력이 좋지는 않지만 사진 찍는 건 좋아해. 참, 몇 달 전에 식당에서 이효리의 사진을 찍었어.
글렌　실물이 더 예뻤어?
제니　응. 실물이 사진보다 낫더라고. 나중에 보여 줄게.

Learn More

1. **If the pictures turn out well, I'd like to have them enlarged.**
   사진이 잘 나온다면 확대하고 싶어.

2. **I'm camera-shy.** 나는 사진 찍기를 싫어해.

unit 21 | What kind of musical was it?
어떤 종류의 뮤지컬이었는데?

Dialog

Eileen My brother gave me tickets for a hip-hop concert. Would you like to come with me?

Victor Wow, that would be very exciting. I'd be glad to go with you.

Eileen The concert is on Saturday at 7:30 p.m. Why don't we meet before the concert to have dinner together?

Victor That's a good idea. Dinner's on me. What kind of food do you want for dinner?

Eileen There is a very good Italian restaurant near the concert hall. I've been there with my family, and my parents liked that place very much.

Victor Okay. Let's go there around 6:00 p.m. I'll make a reservation for us.

Eileen I saw a musical last month, and it was great.

Victor What kind of musical was it?

Eileen It was a Broadway musical. The director was a very famous person from New York.

---

make a reservation 예약하다   director 연출가, 감독

Situation Drill Level 3

Let's Speak!

아일린   우리 형이 힙합 콘서트 티켓을 줬어. 같이 갈래?
빅터   와, 재미있겠다. 같이 가고 싶어.
아일린   콘서트는 토요일 오후 7시 반이야. 콘서트 전에 만나서 저녁 같이 먹는 게 어때?
빅터   좋은 생각이다. 저녁은 내가 살게. 저녁으로 무슨 음식을 먹을래?
아일린   콘서트 장 근처에 맛있는 이탈리아 식당이 있어. 전에 식구들과 갔었는데 부모님께서 굉장히 좋아하셨어.
빅터   좋아. 6시쯤에 가자. 내가 예약을 해 놓을게.
아일린   지난 달엔 뮤지컬을 봤는데 정말 멋있었어.
빅터   어떤 종류의 뮤지컬이었는데?
아일린   브로드웨이 뮤지컬이었어. 연출가가 뉴욕 출신의 유명한 사람이었어.

Learn More

1. **When will the performance be finished?**   공연이 몇 시쯤 끝날까?

2. **Will you show us to our seats?**   저희 좌석으로 안내해 주시겠어요?

3. **I have no ear for music.**   나는 음악을 잘 몰라요.

4. **Do you often go to the theater?**   극장에 자주 가나요?

unit 22 | I'll call the roll first.
우선 출석을 부를게.

Dialog

Teacher   I'll call the roll first. Glen?
Glen   I'm here.
Teacher   Victor?
Glen   He's absent.
Teacher   Do you know why he's absent?
Glen   He's sick. I heard that he went to the hospital this morning.
Teacher   Okay. I'll talk to him later. Jenny? Is Jenny also absent?
Jenny   Oh, I'm sorry.
Teacher   Why are you late?
Jenny   I got up late and missed the bus.
Teacher   Try not to be late next time. And, as your punishment, I want you to erase the blackboard after class. Now, let's start class. Where did we stop last time?
Glen   We finished chapter 3 last time.
Teacher   Let's begin with chapter 4 today. Have you prepared for today's lesson?

---

roll 출석
punishment 벌, 벌칙
absent 결석의, 결근의
blackboard 칠판

Situation Drill Level 3

Let's Speak!

선생님 우선 출석을 부를게. 글렌?
글렌 네.
선생님 빅터?
글렌 결석입니다.
선생님 왜 결석인지 아니?
글렌 아파요. 아침에 병원에 갔다고 들었어요.
선생님 그래. 나중에 빅터랑 얘기할게. 제니? 제니도 결석이니?
제니 죄송합니다.
선생님 왜 늦었니?
제니 늦게 일어나서 버스를 놓쳤어요.
선생님 다음엔 늦지 않도록 해. 그리고 벌로 수업 후 칠판을 지우도록. 수업 시작합시다. 지난 번에 어디까지 했었지?
글렌 지난 시간에 3과를 마쳤습니다.
선생님 그럼 오늘은 4과를 시작하자. 오늘 수업 예습은 해왔니?

Learn More

1. **Do you have any questions about today's lesson?**
   오늘 수업에 대해 질문 있나요?

2. **That's all for today. For homework, I want you to go over what we learned today. And read pages 25-27 before you come to the next class.**
   오늘은 여기까지다. 숙제로는 오늘 배운 부분들을 복습해오거라. 그리고 다음 수업 오기 전에 25-27쪽까지 읽어오거라.

unit 23 | Are you ready for the exam?
시험 공부 많이 했니?

Dialog

Glen   Are you ready for the exam?

Jenny   No. I think I have to cram for the midterm tonight.

Glen   I'm not fully prepared for it either. I have to get a good grade this time because I got a low grade on the last exam.

Jenny   What grade did you get on the last exam?

Glen   I only got a 60 on the last exam. My parents were disappointed in me. So I've been up late the past couple of nights. But I'm still weak at English.

Jenny   Why don't we stay up all night and go over the books together? I'm strong at English, so I can help you with it.

Glen   Oh, really? Thanks a lot. Then I'll give you a hand with mathematics.

---

cram 벼락공부
grade 점수
give a hand 도와 주다

midterm 중간고사
be disappointed in ~에 실망하다

Situation Drill Level 3

Let's Speak!

글렌　시험 공부 많이 했니?
제니　아니. 나 오늘 밤에 중간고사 벼락치기 해야 할 것 같다.
글렌　나도 충분히 준비가 안 됐어. 지난 시험에서 낮은 점수를 받아서 이번엔 좋은 성적을 받아야만 해.
제니　지난 시험에서 몇 점이나 받았는데?
글렌　지난 시험에서 겨우 60점 받았었어. 부모님께서 실망이 크셨어. 그래서 지난 며칠 동안 밤 늦게까지 공부했어. 하지만 아직도 영어에 자신이 없어.
제니　우리 같이 밤 새서 공부하는 게 어때? 난 영어에 자신이 있으니 내가 도와 줄게.
글렌　오, 정말? 너무 고마워. 그럼 나는 수학 공부를 도와 줄게.

Learn More

1. **It's on everything we've learned so far.**
   우리가 지금까지 배운 것 모두가 범위야.

2. **When is the final?** 언제가 기말고사야?

3. **Did you pass the exam?** 그 시험에 합격했니?

unit 24 | I messed up the exam.
나 시험 망쳤어.

Dialog

Eileen How did you do on your exam?

Victor I messed up the exam.

Eileen Oh, I'm sorry to hear that. But you always get good grades in English.

Victor Well, English is my favorite subject, but I didn't get a good grade this time because I got so nervous before the exam. What about you? Did you get a perfect score on the English test?

Eileen I'm not sure whether I got a perfect score on the subjective questions or not.

Victor Our English teacher is very generous with grades, so don't worry too much.

Eileen I hope you're right. Anyway, I feel so relieved that the test is over.

Victor Me, too. How about going to a movie tonight?

---

mess up 망치다
perfect score 만점
generous 관대한

nervous 긴장한
subjective 주관식의
relieved 긴장이 풀어진, 가뿐한

Situation Drill Level 3

Let's Speak!

아일린 시험은 어떻게 봤니?
빅터 망쳤어.
아일린 오, 안됐구나. 하지만 너 영어 점수는 항상 좋잖아.
빅터 음, 영어는 내가 제일 좋아하는 과목이지만 시험 전에 너무 긴장해서 이번엔 잘 못 봤어. 너는 어때? 영어를 만점 받았니?
아일린 주관식 문제를 다 맞았는지 확실하지가 않아.
빅터 우리 영어 선생님께서는 점수를 후하게 주시니 너무 걱정하지 마.
아일린 네 말이 맞았음 좋겠다. 아무튼, 시험이 끝나서 너무 홀가분하다.
빅터 나도 그래. 오늘 밤 영화 보러 가는 게 어때?

Learn More

1. **I've got butterflies in my stomach.** 나 너무 긴장돼.

2. **The math teacher is so picky.** 수학 선생님은 너무 깐깐하셔.

3. **I think I need to take a make-up test.** 나는 재시험을 봐야 할 것 같아.

unit 25 | We're running out of gas.
휘발유가 다 떨어져가네.

Dialog

Eileen   Dad, can you give me a ride to the theater?

Dad   No problem. I'll take you there. Hop in. You should always fasten your seatbelt as soon as you get in the car. Seatbelts save lives.

Eileen   Okay, Dad. This seatbelt is too tight. How can I loosen it?

Dad   Let me help you with that. Here you go. Do you feel comfortable now?

Eileen   Thank you. I feel much more comfortable. By the way, can I change the CD?

Dad   Sure. The other CDs are in the console. Oh, we're running out of gas. I think we need to stop by the gas station.

Eileen   There's a gas station over there. Let's fill up there.

---

hop in (자동차에) 올라타다
tight 꼭 끼는, 꽉 죄는
console (운전석과 조수석 사이에 있는) 콘솔
gas 휘발유

fasten one's seatbelt 안전벨트를 매다
loosen 느슨하게 하다
run out of ~을 다 써버리다
fill up 기름을 가득 채우다

Situation Drill Level 3

Let's Speak!

아일린   아빠, 극장까지 좀 태워다 주실 수 있으세요?
아빠   물론이지. 데려다 주마. 타렴. 항상 차에 타자마자 벨트를 매려무나. 안전벨트는 생명을 구한단다.
아일린   네, 아빠. 벨트가 너무 조여요. 느슨하게 하려면 어떻게 해야 해요?
아빠   내가 도와 줄게. 됐다. 이젠 좀 편하니?
아일린   고맙습니다. 훨씬 편해졌어요. 근데 CD 좀 바꿔도 돼요?
아빠   물론이지. 다른 CD들은 콘솔 안에 있다. 어, 휘발유가 다 떨어져가네. 주유소에 좀 들러야겠다.
아일린   저기 주유소가 있어요. 저기서 기름을 넣어요.

Learn More

1. **Do you need a ride?** 태워다 줄까?

2. **Kill the radio. I can't stand that music.**
   라디오 좀 꺼주세요. 그 음악 너무 이상해요.

3. **Could you speed up?** 빨리 좀 가주실래요?

unit 26 | Where are you headed?
어디 가니?

Dialog

Glen   Where are you headed?

Jenny   I'm going to a travel agency to get a ticket to Toronto.

Glen   Wow. That sounds great. Is that for your summer vacation?

Jenny   Yeah, I'm visiting my uncle in Toronto for 2 weeks.

Glen   Do you need to apply for a passport and visa?

Jenny   No. I don't need a visa, and I already have a passport. Oh, I have to hurry because I need to get to the bank, too.

Glen   You'd better use traveler's checks there. Then you can't lose your money.

Jenny   Thanks for the tip. I'll get a nice souvenir for you from Toronto.

---

travel agency 여행사   **apply** 신청하다
tip 조언   **souvenir** 기념품

Situation Drill Level 3

Let's Speak!

글렌   어디 가니?
제니   토론토행 티켓을 받으러 여행사에 가는 길이야.
글렌   와. 좋겠다. 여름 휴가로 가는 거니?
제니   응, 2주 동안 토론토에 계신 삼촌에게 갈 예정이야.
글렌   여권과 비자를 신청해야 돼?
제니   아니, 비자는 필요 없고 여권은 이미 가지고 있어. 아, 은행도 들러야 하니 서둘러야겠어.
글렌   여행자 수표를 사용하는 것이 좋을 거야. 분실 염려가 없으니 말이야.
제니   정보 고마워. 토론토에서 멋진 기념품을 사다 줄게.

Learn More

1. **Do you take traveler's checks?** 여행자 수표를 받습니까?

2. **You'd better bring along some Korean food.**
   한국 음식을 좀 가져가는 것이 좋을 거야.

3. **I hope you have an unforgettable vacation.**
   잊지 못할 휴기가 되길 비례.

unit 27 | Is it close by?
여기서 가깝나요?

Dialog

Stranger   Excuse me. I'm a stranger here. Are there any subway stations around here?

Glen   Yes, there's one near here.

Stranger   Is it close by?

Glen   It's within walking distance.

Stranger   Then could you tell me how to get to that subway station?

Glen   Sure. Go two more blocks, and then turn right. It's just around the corner. You can't miss it.

Stranger   How long will it take to get there?

Glen   About 15 minutes on foot, I guess.

Stranger   Thank you so much.

---

close by 바로 곁에   **walking distance** 걸어서 갈 수 있는 거리
on foot 걸어서

Situation Drill Level 3

Let's Speak!

외지인　실례합니다. 저는 여기가 처음이라서요. 이 근처에 지하철 역이 있나요?
글렌　　네. 근처에 하나 있습니다.
외지인　여기서 가깝나요?
글렌　　걸어서 갈 만한 거리입니다.
외지인　그럼 그 지하철 역에 어떻게 갈 수 있는지 알려 주시겠어요?
글렌　　물론이죠. 두 블록을 더 가서 오른쪽으로 돌면 바로 모퉁이에 있습니다. 쉽게 찾을 수 있습니다.
외지인　거기까지 가는 데 얼마나 걸릴까요?
글렌　　걸어서 약 15분 정도 걸릴 겁니다.
외지인　고맙습니다.

Learn More

1. **Is it far from here?** 여기서 먼가요?

2. **I don't know which way to go.** 어느 길로 가야 할지 모르겠어요.

3. **How far is it from here to the convenience store?**
   여기서 편의점까지는 거리가 얼마나 되나요?

4. **This is the shortest way to the station.**
   이 길이 역으로 가는 지름길입니다.

unit 28 | It's been a long time.
진짜 오랜만이다.

Dialog

Glen   Excuse me. Don't I know you?

Monica   You look familiar to me, but I'm not sure. Where did you go to elementary school?

Glen   I went to Daejo Elementary School.

Monica   Glen, is that you?

Glen   Monica? Wow, it's been a long time.

Monica   Long time no see. It's already been 7 years since we graduated from school. How have you been?

Glen   I've been good. You haven't changed a bit. You look exactly the same as in elementary school.

Monica   Anyway, what brings you here?

Glen   Oh, I'm here to visit my grandfather. Let's get together again soon.

---

familiar 낯익은
a bit 조금

graduate 졸업하다
get together 만나다

Situation Drill Level 3

Let's Speak!

글렌　실례지만 제가 아는 분이 아닌가요?
모니카　낯이 익긴 한데 잘 모르겠네요. 초등학교를 어디서 다니셨어요?
글렌　대조 초등학교에 다녔어요.
모니카　너 글렌이니?
글렌　모니카? 와, 진짜 오래간만이다.
모니카　오래간만이야. 졸업한 지 벌써 7년이나 지났으니 말이야. 그 동안 어떻게 지 냈니?
글렌　잘 지냈어. 너는 하나도 안 변했구나. 초등학교 다닐 때랑 똑같아.
모니카　그나저나, 여긴 어쩐 일이야?
글렌　어, 할아버지 댁에 가려고 왔어. 언제 다시 한번 보자.

Learn More

1. **It's really good to see you again.**　다시 만나서 정말 반가워.

2. **I haven't seen you around in a while. Where have you been?**
한동안 안 보이던데, 어디 있었니?

3. **You sure have changed.**　너 진짜 많이 변했구나.

unit 29 | How often does the subway come? 지하철은 얼마나 자주 오나요?

Dialog

Visitor   Which line should I take to City Hall?

Eileen   You should take line number 2.

Visitor   You mean I have to transfer subway lines? Where should I change trains to get to City Hall?

Eileen   Go 3 more stops, and then transfer to line number 2.

Visitor   Is it easy to find the way to line number 2?

Eileen   Every transfer station is full of passengers changing trains. But the signs should show you where to go.

Visitor   How often does the subway come?

Eileen   It comes every 5 minutes during the day, but it rarely runs at night.

---

transfer 환승하다, 갈아타다   **passenger** 탑승자
rarely 드물게

Situation Drill Level 3

Let's Speak!

방문객　시청으로 가려면 몇 호선을 타야 하나요?
아일린　2호선을 타야 해요.
방문객　그럼 지하철을 갈아타야 한다는 말인가요? 시청으로 가려면 어디서 갈아 타야 하나요?
아일린　세 정거장 더 가서 2호선으로 갈아타세요.
방문객　2호선으로 갈아타는 길을 찾는 것은 쉽나요?
아일린　환승역마다 갈아타려는 승객들로 붐벼요. 하지만 표지판에 써 있을 겁니다.
방문객　지하철은 얼마나 자주 오나요?
아일린　낮엔 5분마다 다니는데 밤엔 간격이 깁니다.

Learn More

1. **Can you tell me what the next station is, please?**
   다음은 무슨 역인지 알려 주실래요?

2. **The subways are really crowded during rush hour.**
   출퇴근 시간에는 지하철이 너무 붐벼요.

3. **Which exit should I use?** 어느 출구로 나가야 하나요?

unit 30 | May I take your order now?
지금 주문하시겠어요?

Dialog

Eileen We don't have a reservation. How long is the wait for 2 people?

Waiter You can have a seat right away. Would you like a seat by the window?

Eileen That would be great.

Waiter May I take your order now?

Eileen I haven't made up my mind yet. What is today's special?

Waiter Today we have a New York steak and salmon steak. They are pretty popular dishes at our restaurant.

Eileen Sounds good. We'll each try one of them. How long will it take?

Waiter It won't take too long. How would you like the steak cooked?

Eileen Medium well, please.

---

right away 즉시
salmon 연어

make up one's mind 마음의 결정을 내리다

Situation Drill Level 3

Let's Speak!

아일린   예약을 하지 않았는데, 2명 자리는 얼마나 기다려야 하나요?
웨이터   지금 자리가 있습니다. 창가 쪽 자리를 드릴까요?
아일린   좋습니다.
웨이터   지금 주문하시겠어요?
아일린   아직 못 골랐어요. 오늘의 특별 요리는 무엇인가요?
웨이터   오늘은 뉴욕 스테이크와 연어 스테이크가 있습니다. 둘 다 저희 식당에서 꽤 유명한 음식들입니다.
아일린   좋습니다. 하나씩 주문하겠습니다. 음식이 얼마나 걸리나요?
웨이터   그렇게 오래 걸리지는 않을 것입니다. 스테이크는 얼만큼 익혀드릴까요?
아일린   중간보다는 좀더 익혀 주세요.

Learn More

1. **What would you like to drink?**   음료는 무엇으로 드시겠습니까?

2. **There are too many choices on this menu.**
   메뉴 종류가 너무 많군요.

3. **Excuse me, but this isn't what I ordered.**
   저기요, 이건 제가 시킨 음식이 아닌데요.

unit 31 | I can't eat another bite.
더 이상은 못 먹겠어.

Dialog

Glen   It was a delicious meal. I can't eat another bite.

Jenny   Me neither. I think we have to wrap up what's left.

Glen   Waiter, could you wrap this up for us and get the check, please?

Jenny   How much is it?

Glen   Don't worry about it. It's on me.

Jenny   Oh, really? Thank you. I'll get it next time.

Glen   Oh, I think they charged us for something we didn't have. Excuse me. I think there's a mistake on this bill. We didn't order any dessert.

Waiter   Oh, we're terribly sorry. We'll get you the correct bill right away.

---

bite 한 입, 물기
check 계산서(= bill)
wrap up 포장해 가다

Situation Drill Level 3

Let's Speak!

글렌   맛있는 식사였어. 더 이상은 못 먹겠어.
제니   나도 그래. 남은 음식을 포장해 가야 할 것 같아.
글렌   웨이터, 이 음식을 포장해 주시고 계산서 좀 주실래요?
제니   얼마 나왔어?
글렌   걱정 마. 내가 낼게.
제니   정말? 고마워. 다음엔 내가 살게.
글렌   어, 우리가 주문하지 않은 것을 계산한 것 같아. 여기요. 계산서에 실수가 있는 것 같아요. 우리는 디저트를 주문하지 않았어요.
웨이터   아, 정말 죄송합니다. 제대로 된 계산서를 바로 가져다 드리겠습니다.

Learn More

1. **Let's go Dutch.** 각자 지불하도록 하자.

2. **Let's split the bill.** 계산은 각자 부담하자.

3. **I'd really like to have some dessert, but I can't eat any more.**
후식을 먹고 싶지만 더 이상은 못 먹겠어.

unit 32 | This book is out now.
이 책은 대출 중입니다.

Dialog

Eileen Excuse me. Where can I find this geography book?

Librarian Go to the second floor, and check section B.

Eileen I've already checked there, but I can't find the book.

Librarian Then write down the title of the book and the name of the author. I'll look for it on the computer. Oh, I got it. This book is out now.

Eileen Oh, no. I need that book for tomorrow's homework. When will it be returned?

Librarian Let me check. This book should be returned today. Would you like to reserve it?

Eileen Yes, please.

Librarian Show me your student ID. And don't forget we close at 8 in the evening, so you should check before then.

---

geography 지리학   **author** 저자

Situation Drill Level 3

Let's Speak!

아일린 실례합니다. 이 지리학 책을 어디서 찾을 수 있을까요?
사서 2층으로 가서 B 섹션을 확인해 보세요.
아일린 이미 가봤는데 책을 못 찾겠어서요.
사서 그럼 책 제목과 저자를 써주세요. 컴퓨터로 찾아 볼게요.
 여기 있군요. 이 책은 대출 중입니다.
아일린 아, 이런. 내일 숙제를 위해 그 책이 필요한데. 언제 반납될 예정인가요?
사서 확인해 보겠습니다. 이 책은 오늘까지 반납될 예정이군요. 책을 예약하시겠어요?
아일린 네, 그럴게요.
사서 학생증을 보여 주세요. 그리고 도서관은 밤 8시에 닫으니 그 전에 꼭 확인하세요.

Learn More

1. **You should return the book by this Friday.**
 이번 금요일까지는 책을 반환해야 합니다.

2. **If you don't have your student ID, you can't borrow any books here.** 학생증이 없으면 어떤 책도 빌릴 수 없습니다.

unit 33 | What seems to be the problem?
어디가 아프신가요?

Dialog

Glen I have a 2 o'clock appointment to see Dr. Stevenson.

Nurse I'll check the chart. Here you are. The doctor is with another patient now. Please have a seat over there, and then the doctor will be with you shortly.

Dr. Stevenson What seems to be the problem?

Glen I'm having stomach pains. My stomach has been hurting for a few days.

Dr. Stevenson Have you ever had these symptoms before?

Glen No. And I also have diarrhea.

Dr. Stevenson I think you have mild food poisoning. I'll prescribe a day's worth of medicine.

---

stomach 배, 위
diarrhea 설사
prescribe 처방하다
symptom 증상
food poisoning 식중독

Situation Drill Level 3

Let's Speak!

글렌   2시에 스티븐슨 선생님과 진찰 예약을 해놓았는데요.
간호사   차트를 확인해 보지요. 여기 있네요. 지금 선생님이 다른 환자를 진찰 중이십니다. 저기 앉아서 기다리시면 선생님께서 곧 진료를 봐주실 겁니다.
스티븐슨 어디가 아프신가요?
글렌   배가 아파요. 며칠 동안 계속 아팠어요.
스티븐슨 예전에 이런 증상이 있었나요?
글렌   아니요. 그리고 또 설사를 해요.
스티븐슨 가벼운 식중독에 걸린 것 같군요. 하루치 약을 지어 드리겠습니다.

Learn More

1. **Have your temperature and blood pressure been checked?**
   체온과 혈압은 쟀나요?

2. **Did you follow the doctor's instructions?**   의사의 지시를 따랐나요?

3. **I've got a lot of gas.**   속에 가스가 찼어요.

unit 34 | Could you fill this prescription for me? 약을 조제해 주시겠어요?

Dialog

Eileen   I have a prescription from my doctor. Could you fill this prescription for me?

Pharmacist   I'll take care of it right away. Take one tablet three times a day after each meal, and take two pills before going to bed.

Eileen   Will this make me drowsy?

Pharmacist   This'll make you dizzy, so you must take this medicine after meals.

Eileen   Can I get something that won't make me sleepy?

Pharmacist   I'm sorry. We can't give you that medicine without a prescription, and it's not as strong.

Eileen   I see. I also cut my finger. I need some antibiotic cream and Band-Aids.

---

prescription 처방, 처방약
drowsy 졸린, 어지러운
antibiotic cream 항생 연고
tablet 알약(= pill)
dizzy 어지러운

Situation Drill Level 3

Let's Speak!

아일린 의사 선생님께서 주신 처방전이 있습니다. 약을 조제해 주시겠어요?
약사   바로 조제해 드리겠습니다. 하루 세 번, 식후에 한 알씩 드시고 주무시기 전에 두 알씩 복용하세요.
아일린 이 약을 먹으면 졸음이 오나요?
약사   이 약을 먹으면 어지러울 것이기 때문에 꼭 식후에 드셔야 합니다.
아일린 졸리지 않는 약으로 지을 수는 없나요?
약사   죄송합니다. 처방전 없이는 그 약을 지을 수 없고, 그리 효과가 좋지도 않습니다.
아일린 알겠습니다. 손가락도 베었거든요. 항생 연고와 밴드를 주세요.

Learn More

1. **This should clear it right up.** 이 약을 드시면 바로 해결될 겁니다.

2. **Have you had any prescriptions filled here before?**
   저희 약국에서 조제받으신 적이 있습니까?

3. **I don't know what to choose. Can you recommend something for a migraine?**
   무엇을 골라야 할지 모르겠어요. 편두통 약을 추천해 주시겠어요?

unit 35 | How would you like to have your hair done? 머리를 어떻게 해드릴까요?

Dialog

Designer How would you like to have your hair done?

Eileen I want a haircut, and also I want to get a perm.

Designer I'll give you a trim and then a shampoo.

Eileen Don't cut it too short or too long. I always tie my hair in the back. But I want to change my hairstyle this time.

Designer What did you have in mind?

Eileen Nothing special.

Designer Then what about having bangs after you get a perm? Oh, I'll show you some pictures of people with bangs.

Eileen Thank you. And I want just a little curl at the ends of my hair.

---

get a perm 파마하다
tie 묶다
trim 다듬다, 손질하다
bangs 앞머리

Situation Drill Level 3

Let's Speak!

디자이너   머리를 어떻게 해드릴까요?
아일린   머리를 깎고 파마도 해주세요.
디자이너   머리를 다듬은 다음 샴푸를 하겠습니다.
아일린   길이는 적당히 잘라 주세요. 항상 머리를 뒤로 묶었는데, 이번엔 스타일을 좀 바꾸려구요.
디자이너   생각해 둔 스타일이 있으세요?
아일린   특별히 없어요.
디자이너   파마 후에 앞머리를 자르는 것은 어때요? 아, 앞머리 사진들을 좀 보여 드릴게요.
아일린   고맙습니다. 그리고 머리 끝부분만 곱슬거리게 파마해 주세요.

Learn More

1. **You've got thick hair. I'll thin it out for you.**
   머리숱이 많으시네요. 숱을 좀 쳐내 드릴게요.

2. **Should I leave it this length?** 이 길이로 그냥 남겨 둘까요?

3. **Don't put any wax in my hair, please.**
   머리에 왁스 같은 거 바르지 말아 주세요.

4. **I don't want to have a part in my hair.** 가르마는 타고 싶지 않아요.

unit 36 | I'd like to open an account.
은행 계좌를 열고 싶은데요.

Dialog

Glen   I'd like to open an account.

Clerk   Okay. Please complete this application for a new account.

Glen   If I need to use checks, what kind of account should I choose?

Clerk   You might want to choose a checking account. And I need to see your ID.

Glen   Here it is. Is there anything else I should do?

Clerk   Yes. Please write down your secret number here. Then that's it.

Glen   Oh, I almost forgot. Will you please cash this check for me?

Clerk   Sure. Just endorse your check, please.

---

account 계좌   **application** 신청서
secret number 비밀번호 (= PIN)   **cash** 현금으로 바꾸다
endorse 이서하다

Situation Drill Level 3

Let's Speak!

글렌　　은행 계좌를 열고 싶은데요.
은행원　네. 새 계좌를 여시려면 이 신청서를 작성해 주세요.
글렌　　수표를 써야 하면, 어떤 계좌를 선택해야 하나요?
은행원　당좌 계좌를 선택하시면 됩니다. 그리고 신분증을 좀 보여 주세요.
글렌　　여기 있습니다. 더 해야 할 것이 있나요?
은행원　네. 여기에 비밀번호를 적어 주세요. 그럼 끝납니다.
글렌　　아, 잊을 뻔했네요. 이 수표를 현금으로 좀 바꿔 주시겠어요?
은행원　물론이죠. 수표에 이서만 좀 해주세요.

Learn More

1. **I would like to make a deposit into my saving account.**
   제 저축계좌에 예금을 하고 싶습니다.

2. **The ATM ate my card.** 현금자동지급기가 내 카드를 삼켰어.

3. **I'd like to close my account.** 제 계좌를 해지하고 싶습니다.

4. **How do I withdraw money?** 돈은 어떻게 인출합니까?

5. **There's a service charge for using a different bank's ATM.**
   다른 은행의 현금자동지급기를 사용하면 수수료가 부과됩니다.

unit 37 | Are you a Christian?
너 기독교 신자니?

Dialog

Jeeny   What are you doing on Sunday? Let's go hiking.

Glen   I'm afraid I can't. I have to go to church.

Jeeny   Are you a Christian?

Glen   Yes. I go to church every Sunday. Do you attend church services?

Jeeny   No, I don't. I'm a Buddhist. Since when have you attended church services?

Glen   My mother used to send my sister and me to Sunday school when I was young.

Jeeny   What time is the service on Sunday?

Glen   The service starts at eleven o'clock in the morning, and it ends around twelve thirty. Then let's go hiking on Sunday in the afternoon.

---

attend 참석하다   **church services** 교회 예배
Buddhist 불교신자

Situation Drill Level 3

Let's Speak!

제니   이번 일요일에 뭐하니? 하이킹 가자!
글렌   유감스럽지만 안 돼. 교회에 가야 하거든.
제니   너 기독교 신자니?
글렌   응. 난 일요일마다 교회에 가. 교회 예배 드리니?
제니   아니. 난 불교신자야. 언제부터 예배를 드렸었니?
글렌   어렸을 때 어머니께서 나와 내 여동생을 주일 학교에 보내셨어.
제니   일요일에 예배가 몇 시니?
글렌   예배는 오전 11시에 시작해서 12시 반 정도에 끝나. 그럼 일요일 오후에 하이킹 가자.

Learn More

1. **They believe in God.** 그들은 신이 있다고 믿습니다.

2. **I enjoy listening to the organ and the choir.**
   난 오르간과 성가대 합창 듣는 것을 좋아해.

unit 38 | This is my first time to take a plane. 비행기 타는 건 처음이야.

Dialog

Victor: I think our seats are here.

Glen: This is my first time to take a plane.

Victor: You must be very excited.

Glen: No, I'm afraid of flying. I only want to get there in one piece.

Flight Attendant: Ladies and gentlemen, we will now begin our meal service. Your choices are chicken and fish. Which would you like to have?

Glen: I'll have the fish, please.

Flight Attendant: Would you like something to drink?

Glen: Coke, please. Oh, do you have anything for airsickness? I'm not feeling well.

Flight Attendant: I'll get you some medicine and an airsickness bag.

---

in one piece 무사히
airsickness 비행기 멀미

motion sickness 멀미

Situation Drill Level 3

Let's Speak!

빅터　여기가 우리 자리인 것 같아.
글렌　비행기 타는 건 이번이 처음이야.
빅터　너 굉장히 흥분되겠구나.
글렌　아니, 난 비행기 타는 게 무서워. 무사히 도착만 했음 좋겠어.
승무원　여러분, 지금부터 식사를 제공해 드리도록 하겠습니다. 닭고기나 생선 요리를 선택하실 수 있습니다. 어떤 것으로 드릴까요?
글렌　생선 요리로 하겠습니다.
승무원　마실 것을 좀 드릴까요?
글렌　콜라 주세요. 아, 멀미약으로 뭐가 좀 있나요? 몸이 좀 안 좋네요.
승무원　멀미약과 멀미용 봉투를 가져다 드리겠습니다.

Learn More

1. **Would you care for some nuts?** 땅콩을 드시겠어요?

2. **I'm sorry, but I believe this is my seat.**
   죄송합니다만 여기는 제 자리인 것 같습니다.

unit 39 | This package contains books and pictures.
이 소포의 내용물은 책과 사진들입니다.

Dialog

Glen I want to send this package to Boston. Is this size all right?

Clerk The size is okay. What's in the package?

Glen This package contains books and pictures. How much is it to send it internationally?

Clerk That depends on its weight. Will you please weigh that package?

Glen This package needs to get to Boston by tomorrow. So I'd like to send this package by airmail.

Clerk Okay. Then it will be more expensive than sending it by boat. Would you like to insure the contents?

Glen No. That won't be necessary.

Clerk The price is fifteen thousand won. Here's your receipt.

---

package 소포
depend on ~에 달려있다
contain 담고 있다, 포함하다
insure 보험을 들다

Situation Drill Level 3

Let's Speak!

글렌　이 소포를 보스턴으로 보내고 싶습니다. 이만한 사이즈는 괜찮겠죠?
직원　사이즈는 괜찮습니다. 소포 안에는 무엇이 있습니까?
글렌　소포 안에는 책과 사진들이 들어 있습니다. 국제 우편 발송은 얼마입니까?
직원　무게에 따라 다릅니다. 소포의 무게를 달아 주시겠어요?
글렌　이 소포는 내일까지 보스턴에 도착해야 합니다. 그래서 비행기로 보내고 싶은데요.
직원　알겠습니다. 그럼 배로 보내는 것보다는 더 비쌉니다. 내용물에 대한 보험을 들고 싶습니까?
글렌　아니요. 그렇게까지는 필요하지 않아요.
직원　15,000원입니다. 여기 영수증 받으세요.

Learn More

1. **When will it reach New York?** 언제 뉴욕에 도착합니까?

2. **I want to send this postal card by registered mail.**
   이 엽서를 등기우편으로 보내 주세요.

3. **How long will it take to get there?**
   우편물이 그곳에 도착하려면 얼마나 걸립니까?

unit 40 | Do you have any particular style in mind? 특별히 생각해 두신 스타일이 있나요?

Dialog

Salesman Can I help you find something?

Eileen Yes, I'm looking for a T-shirt.

Salesman Do you have any particular style in mind?

Eileen No. Can you recommend something for me?

Salesman This is the latest style. What size do you wear?

Eileen I'm a size 6. Can I try it on?

Salesman Sure. The fitting rooms are over there.

Eileen I like it very much. There's no price tag on this. How much is this?

Salesman Its original price was 30,000 won, but I can give you 20% off on it. This is a good buy.

Eileen Okay. I'll take it.

---

latest 최근의   price tag 가격표

Situation Drill Level 3

Let's Speak!

판매원 뭘 찾으시는지 도와 드릴까요?
아일린 네, 티셔츠를 찾고 있는데요.
판매원 특별히 생각해 두신 스타일이 있나요?
아일린 아니오. 추천을 좀 해주시겠어요?
판매원 이것은 최근 모델입니다. 사이즈가 어떻게 되시나요?
아일린 사이즈 6입니다. 입어 봐도 되나요?
판매원 물론입니다. 옷 갈아입는 곳은 저쪽입니다.
아일린 옷이 마음에 드는군요. 가격표가 없는데, 얼마입니까?
판매원 원래 가격은 3만원인데 20% 할인을 해드리겠습니다. 이 가격이면 잘 사시는 겁니다.
아일린 좋아요. 사겠어요.

Learn More

1. **On what floor can I buy a swimsuit?** 수영복은 몇 층에서 살 수 있습니까?

2. **How come this store is so high?** 어째서 이 가게는 이렇게 비싼 거지?

3. **Can I wash it by hand?** 손으로 빨아도 됩니까?